WOMEN IN MINISTRY
25 WAYS TO IMPACT THE WORLD

ELEANOR CRAWFORD

WOMEN IN MINISTRY
25 WAYS TO IMPACT THE WORLD

Copyright © by Eleanor Crawford

All rights reserved. No part of this book may be reproduced or transmitted in any form or by any means without written permission of the author.

ISBN 978-0-935379-11-2

Library of Congress Control Number: 2016902849

Published by New Life Educational Services
P.O. Box 96
Oak Lawn, Illinois 60454

Printed in the U.S.A.

Contents

Introduction	1
1. Eve – Bringing Life	3
2. Sarah (Sarai) – Making the Most of the Waiting Time	5
3. Rebekah - Meeting others' needs	7
4. Tamar – Persistence	10
5. Rahab - Hospitality	12
6. Deborah - Role Model of Leadership	14
7. Jael – Strength	16
8. Ruth – Loyalty	17
9. Naomi (Mara) - Honesty	19
10. Hannah – Commitment to Prayer	21
11. Abigail – Diplomacy	23
12. Queen Esther – Compassion	25
13. Elisabeth - Friendship	27
14. Mary – The Mother of Jesus – Obedience	29
15. Anna – Patience	31

16. Bathsheba – Processing Loss   32

17. A Sinful Woman Forgiven – Repentance   34

18. Samaritan woman at the well –
One encounter can change everything   35

- Mary & Martha   37

19. Mary, the sister of Lazarus – Listening to the Word   38

20. Martha, the sister of Lazarus –
Working Together in Ministry   40

21. The Woman Caught in Adultery – Redemption   42

22. Mary Magdalene – Telling your story   44

23. The Woman with the Issue of Blood – Faith   46

24. Lydia - An Open Heart   48

25. Tabitha - Acts of service   50

WOMAN TO WOMAN MINISTRIES   53

OH WOMAN OF MINISTRY   55

FORTHCOMING BOOKS BY ELEANOR CRAWFORD   57

FORTHCOMING BOOKS   59

BY ALPHONSO CRAWFORD   59

FORTHCOMING BOOKS   63

BY BYRON CRAWFORD	63
SIGN UP AND BE NOTIFIED FOR	65
SEMINARS/WORKSHOPS/CONFERENCES	65
SEMINARS/WORKSHOPS/CONFERENCES	67
ABOUT THE AUTHOR	71

Women in Ministry
25 Ways to Impact the World

Introduction

God calls all people to put their faith in Him (Romans 10:11). In turn, He calls all people who put their faith in Him to serve Him (James 2:14-26). There's a familiar Sunday school song that says, "This little light of mine, I'm going to let it shine." This simple song teaches us to share our light (faith) with the world (Matthew 5:15).

The faith we have in the Lord should be translated into action that will impact the world. Every person has been given varying gifts and talents. There are spiritual gifts that we can develop and use for service like prophecy, teaching, encouragement, and giving (Romans 12:4-8). There are also gifts and talents related to our natural tendencies. Some individuals are musically gifted, some are able to make business plans, some are natural leaders, and some are gifted with handling finances. God gives His children a wide spectrum of gifts because there is a lot of work to be done for the kingdom.

Before we begin, talking about how women can impact the world, I want to frame the discussion.

The lives of all christians should be grounded in Scripture and we must follow the example of Christ (1 Corinthians 11:1). Our actions, beliefs, and attitudes should be grounded in His Word, which endures forever (1 Peter 1:25).

The individuals we read about in the bible are products of their time and culture. Keep in mind that their actions were grounded in a social, cultural, familial, religious, and historical context.

When we think about ways women in ministry can impact the world, looking at women in the Bible is an excellent source.

The women who read this book will come from different walks of life: age, marital status, race, education. Please keep in mind that this book is written for a broad audience. It is not designed to limit the reader.

Please ask God to open your heart and mind. Please move forward with an open heart

1. Eve – Bringing Life

God created the world in seven days by speaking the world into being. He created the first man, Adam, in His own image and likeness (Genesis 1:26) by breathing into man's nostrils (2:7). God saw it wasn't good for man to be alone (2:18) so He created Eve from a rib taken from Adam (2:22).

God could've chosen any bone from Adam's body, and God chose the rib, a bone closest to the man's heart. This is a beautiful image of trust and protection for both people in a marriage relationship.

God created women as a vessel to bring life into the world by carrying a child for nine months, giving birth, and nurturing. Eve became the mother of all humanity.

Ways to Impact the World

God created Eve as a partner for Adam . Whether you're single, married, or have children, women can have a profound impact on the world by taking care of the family and friends closest to you. My parents used to say, "You learn love at home."

Like Eve, women have the power to bring life into the world a number of ways:

- Physically giving birth to a child

- Spiritually, through prayer and intercession for those around her

- Emotionally, through words of encouragement

Each one of us has spheres of influence where we have impact and influence. The smallest and tightest circle is usually our immediate family. Your immediate family can be your parents and siblings, your spouse and children. You may also have a close circle of friends that you consider immediate family.

What are some ways you can impact the world?

- Prayer – Pray for your loved ones every day. Keep a list of names on an index card inside your Bible to remind you to pray for them. Be sure to ask loved ones what their prayer concerns are, follow-up with them. Knowing that someone is praying for me is empowering!

- Apologize and forgive – We are all human beings with failings. We make mistakes. God asks us to forgive others as He has forgiven us. Be honest with your loved ones if you mess up, take responsibility for your actions. Seek reconciliation and move forward.

- Put your love into action – Take time to consider the needs of people around you. It will depend on the situation you are in. Pay attention to what your loved ones need (Help with the laundry? A little quiet time?) and offer to help if possible.

2. Sarah (Sarai) – Making the Most of the Waiting Time

I want to set up historical context for Sarah's story. At that time, people traveled from place to place living in tents. The strength and wealth of a family was in their numbers: wives, children, servants, and herds. Sarah was barren (Genesis 11:30), or unable to give her husband children. That meant that when Abraham died, his wealth and property would be passed to the closest male relative.

God told Abraham in Genesis 12:2 that He would make Abraham a great nation. Abraham's descendants would be more numerous than the stars (Genesis 15:5). And he was married to a barren woman. I'm contemplating the conversations Abraham and Sarah must've had over the years. Unfortunately, Sarah tried taking God's promise into her own hands and asked Hagar to have her child (Genesis 16). Many people had to contend with the consequences of these actions.

God's promise was brought into fruition. Sarah was around 90 years old when she became the mother of Isaac (Genesis 17:17)! The faith of Abraham and Sarah led them to an inheritance (Hebrews 11:8-12). Today the jewish people are Abrahams descendants; christians are his spiritual descendants (Galatians 3:29).

Ways to Impact the World

Our situation today is different than Abraham and Sarah's. We can read through the Word and see how God gave His one and only son to die for our sins. When Christ died, the curtain that held

God's Spirit in the Holy of Holies was torn. We can access God's throne room anytime, anywhere by calling God's name! The Lord spoke to Abraham and told him he would be the father of nations. Today we have the Word of God, which is full of His promises!

Sometimes God asks us to wait before His promises are fulfilled. How can you impact the world from the waiting room? Make the most of waiting time:

- Seek after Him through reading the Word. Allow God to minister to you and strengthen you

- Learn as much as you can from other christians who have gone through similar situations.

- Be honest with God! He already knows that we're going through a spectrum of emotions like anger, loneliness, and frustration. He is there to listen.

- If you feel tempted to take things into your own hands, remember that consequences will follow.

Remember: the promise of God will come to fruition in His time.

3. Rebekah - Meeting others' needs

When Isaac reached the age when he was ready for marriage, Abraham sent a servant back to his home country to find Isaac a wife (Genesis 24:1-4). At that time, arranged marriages were common place to ensure that family lines continued, for political alliances and for business reasons (sharing wealth).

Abraham's servant traveled by camel back to the city of Nahor (24:10-11). Traveling is exhausting and this man was bumping along on the back of a camel, or walking, for days. He was dusty and hot, so seeing the city and the well was a welcome relief. The well and the city meant rest and refreshment. It was a daily chore for the women of the city to come to the well to draw water for their homes (24:13). Abraham's servant approached Rebekah and asked her for a drink of water. She also filled the water trough for the camels to drink. She extended an invitation for the servant to stay at her father's house (24:25). Her father was Abraham's family member (24:27).

The servant told Rebekah's family that her actions were the answer to his prayer to find Abraham's son, Isaac, a wife. (24:58). Rebekah agreed to return to Abraham's family with the servant. She became Isaac's wife and he loved her (24:67).

Ways to Impact the World

Because there were no roadside motels or inns, people traveling through a city relied on the residents there for water, food, and a place to sleep. Inviting a person into the family home brought the traveler under that home's protection. Hospitality was an extremely important value. Rebekah extended hospitality to

Abraham's servant by offering him refreshments; she went the extra mile by providing water for the animals. Her family took the servant in as their guest.

I remember reading about Maslow's Hierarchy of Needs during my Psychology courses. The most basic human needs include Biological and Physiological[1]. Rebekah and her family helped to meet the servant's needs: water drink, food to eat, and a place to sleep. Rebekah and her family opened their home to him and met the servant's safety needs.

Jesus said that when we offer hospitality to someone in need, we do that as unto the Lord (Matthew 10:40-42).

Offering hospitality and comfort is a powerful ministry opportunity. Women often come to one another upset or in distress. I hate to hear people say things like, "Don't be upset!" because that's ignoring very powerful emotions. We can't simply turn off emotions with a switch!

When a friend comes to you I recommend following these steps:

- Make sure your friend has a chance to catch her breath and have a glass of water. Sometimes we need a chance to simply calm down. If you can, offer something to eat and a comfortable place to sit.

- Make sure your friend feels safe. Assure her that you're there to support her. Ask others to give her privacy if necessary.

- Listen. Let your friend talk and listen carefully. Don't

---

1 http://www.simplypsychology.org/maslow.html

be quick to offer advice. I find that people often just need a chance to process.

- Pray with your friend and reassure her that God is always with her.

- Encourage your friend to move forward and make decisions based on the Word of God.

Offering a safe emotional space for a friend can make a huge difference in a difficult situation.

Hospitality is important, but I want to offer this gentle warning: use wisdom. Welcoming a stranger into your home can put you and your family in danger, even if you have good intentions. Sometimes individuals have emotional, mental, spiritual, or physical problems that we cannot handle on our own. Trying to handle this can lead to emotional burn out or toxic relationships. Sometimes the most helpful thing is to say, "Let me help you find other resources." We can find ourselves in a position where we are enabling bad behavior if we try to prevent others from experiencing the consequences of their actions.

If someone is severely depressed or suicidal, please contact a hospital right away. If someone is experiencing abuse, contact the authorities.

4. Tamar – Persistence

The story of Judah and Tamar is found in Genesis 38 in the middle of Joseph's story. Some biblical scholars believe that this shows the contrast between the character of Judah and Joseph[2].

Tamar was the wife of Judah's son Er (Genesis 38:6). Er was a wicked man and God put him to death (38:7). According to the Jewish tradition of the Levirate message a widow would marry the younger brother of her husband. Any children they had would be considered the first son's descendants. Er's brother Onan refused to give Tamar a child (38:8-10). Judah promised that his youngest son, Shelah, would give her a child, but Judah did not keep that promise. Tamar made the decision to disguise herself as a prostitute and met Judah while he was on a trip. Judah gave Tamar some possessions as a kind of security deposit. Tamar became pregnant and she was able to prove that Judah was the father. Tamar gave birth to twins and she is listed in the ancestors of Jesus Christ (Matthew 1:1).

Ways to Impact the World

It's hard to wrap my mind around the actions of Tamar. Her story and circumstances are so far removed from mine that I have a hard time finding common ground.

- Be Persistent---Press through obstacles and oppositions.

---

2 http://jwa.org/encyclopedia/article/tamar-bible

My husband Alphonso always says, "Never give up. Never give up." That anthem echoed in my head in difficult circumstances. Knowing the Lord is with me has given me strength to move forward. When we see God strengthening us in little things, we have confidence in bigger and bigger things.

We impact the world when we move forward and rely on God's strength. When things are accomplished we can say, "I did this by God's strength. To Him be the glory!"

- Be Assertive – A person who is assertive stands up for themselves and makes sure their voice is heard.

Please don't confuse being assertive with being rude. All our actions should be motivated by love!

Christians can walk in confidence tempered with humility. We have confidence because God is with us, but we acknowledge that we're reliant on God.

- Be unconventional – Sometimes we need to be creative in problem solving. Thinking outside the box can be a powerful tool!

God can give us wisdom in dealing with problems. Sometimes the best thing to do is step away from the problem. Pray for the Lord to show you the solution. Praise God when inspiration comes!

5. Rahab[3] - Hospitality

Rahab's story could easily be made into an action move: spies, international intrigue, and danger! At the end of Deuteronomy, the children of Israel reached Canaan. Moses left Joshua the son of Nun in charge (Deuteronomy 34). Joshua was in charge of leading the Israelites into the Promised Land. He sent two spies into Jericho (Joshua 2:1).

The two spies stayed in the home of a woman named Rahab (Joshua 2:2). (Rahab is identified as a prostitute, but scholars suggest that she was an innkeeper.)[4] When the King of Jericho asked her to turn the spies over she lied and said they'd left; in reality, the spies were hiding on her roof. Rahab believed that the Lord was giving the Israelites the land (Joshua 2:9). Rahab asks for the Lord to save her family from the coming destruction (2:12-13). Rahab's house was part of the city wall so she let the spies down from a window so they could escape.

When the Israelites entered the land, Jericho fell and the whole city was destroyed (6:22-27). The spies went into Rahab's home and brought out her whole family to safety. Rahab married Salmon and she is mentioned in Christ's ancestry (Matthew 1:5)

Ways to Impact the World

- Faith - Rahab's actions saved the lives of the Israelite spies[5]. She'd heard about the deliverance of the Israelites out of Egypt across the Red Sea (Joshua 2:10). She

---

3 http://www.christiananswers.net/dictionary/rahab.html
4 http://sbl-site.org/publications/article.aspx?articleId=786
5 http://sbl-site.org/publications/article.aspx?articleId=786

declared that He is "God in the heavens above, and on the earth beneath." (2:11). Rahab heard of God's power through His actions and put her belief in Him.

So many people say, 'I'll believe in God if He sends me a sign.' Rahab believed in God because of His reputation. That takes great courage and trust! Today we have the Word of God and we can talk to God anytime or anywhere!

- Hospitality – Rahab extended hospitality to the spies when she gave them a place to stay. That hospitality became hiding the men, helping them escape, and saving their lives.

  Hospitality isn't always limited to offering someone something to eat or drink. Hospitality means looking out for the welfare and wellbeing of others.

- Mercy – Mercy is treating someone with kindness when they could be treated with disdain. Rahab could have turned the spies over to the King. Maybe she would have received a reward, but then her family would have been lost in the destruction of Jericho (Joshua 6:21).

  Mercy is one of the virtues required of us (Micah 6:8 – He has shown you, O man, what is good; And what does the LORD require of thee, but to do justly, and to love mercy, and to walk humbly with thy God?

Belief in God should compel us to act in ways that honor God. Rahab is an example of what faith should look like in our lives.

6. Deborah[6] - Role Model of Leadership

After Joshua died, Israel was led by men and women named Judges. (After the Judges, King Saul was chosen as the leader of Israel.) Something important to point out is that the Israelites failed to follow God's directives and put the inhabitants of the land to death (Judges 1:27-36). The Lord raised up judges to lead the people (Judges 2:16) and save them from the people of the land, like the Canaanites who were making their lives miserable.

Deborah was a judge of Israel and a prophetess (Judges 4:4-6) who served the people while sitting under a palm tree. Jabin the King of Canaan had the Israelites under his thumb. Deborah instructed Barak to gather 10,000 men to fight against the Canaanite army (led by Sisera). Deborah prophesied that Israel would win the battle (4:14).

Ways to Impact the World

Deborah was raised up by the Lord to be a leader and judge. She is an example of biblical leadership.[7]

- Leadership is a noble desire (1 Timothy 3:1) – Leaders need to understand the weight of the job they're taking on. It requires integrity, and responsibility.

    The Lord raised up judges (Judges 2:16) like Deborah. Her calling was God given. She listened to the Lord and shared His directives with the Israelite leadership.

---

6 http://www.todayschristianwoman.com/articles/2007/march/9.22.html
7 http://www.christianitytoday.com/le/2007/july-online-only/le-040329.html

- Leadership requires commitment (2 Timothy 2:1-13) – Leaders don't get entangled in things that aren't a priority. (An example given in 2 Timothy is that soldiers don't get involved in civilian matters.) The Israelites knew they could find Deborah under the palm tree (Judges 4:5)

- Leaders are an example of faith (Hebrews 13:7) – Leaders impact the lives of others around them and they are a role model.

7. Jael – Strength

Jael's story is part of the battle with Sisera. She was married to Heber the Kenite. The Kenites were a nomadic clan. Sisera was the general of the Canaanite army and he was running away from the battle (Judges 4:17). He came to the tent of Jael thinking it was the tent of an ally. Sisera fell asleep in Jael's tent. When he fell asleep, Jael drove a tent peg into his tent and assassinated him.

Jael was called "Most blessed of women…" (Judges 5:24) because she was a defender of Israel.

Ways to Impact the World

Our culture values strength and independence. We look up to people who show themselves strong in God. Jael showed strength and independence in her actions when Sisera came to her for protection. The strength and independence that Jael showed was based on her desire to defend Israel. Remember that the Lord is our source of strength! (Psalm 28:7) He gives us the things we need in order to serve Him.

---

8   https://en.wikipedia.org/wiki/Jael

8. Ruth – Loyalty[9]

I realize that Ruth is a popular topic of bible studies, and for good reason! The story is that God cares for His people.

Ruth was a young woman from the land of Moab. She traveled back to Bethlehem with her mother-in-law, Naomi, after they were both widowed. Ruth left behind everything familiar to her out of loyalty to Naomi. In Bethlehem, Ruth was forced to glean from the fields to ensure that there was food on the table. Ruth met Boaz when she was gleaning in his field. It turned out that Boaz was Naomi's kinsmen redeemer. The Lord brought Ruth and Boaz together, and they were in the lineage of Jesus.

Ways to Impact the world

The word "loving-kindness" appears in the book of Ruth. It is translated from the Hebrew word *hesed*.[10] It is a special type of love that manifests as loyalty above and beyond expectations.

When Naomi was leaving Moab, she told Ruth and Orpah, her daughters-in-law, to stay in Moab where she could return to her family. Ruth could've walked back into Moab and rejoined her family. Instead, Ruth clung to Naomi and said, "Do not urge me to leave you…" (Ruth 1:16).

We talked before about the tradition of the Levirite marriage (Deuteronomy 25:5-6). A widow could marry her brother-in-law in order to have an heir for her deceased husband. In the book of <u>Ruth, Boaz is</u> in a position to be a "kinsman-redeemer" because

Boaz was a close relative of Naomi's husband (Ruth 2:1). Boaz was a solid guy who stepped in to provide for both Naomi and Ruth!

Loyalty is a way to impact the world. Steadfast love for our family can demonstrate Christ-like love for them. Stand by the people in your life and go above and beyond the "call of duty" to serve them.

9. Naomi (Mara) - Honesty

To understand the context of the book of Ruth, look at Judges 21:25: "In those days there was no king in Israel. Every man did that which was right in his own eyes." To make matters worse, there was a famine in the land (Ruth 1:1). Things were so bad for Elimelech, his wife Naomi, and their sons. They went to live in Moab. Moab was made up of the descendants of Lot's sons (Genesis 19:37-38). Naomi's sons both married Moabite women, Ruth and Orpah. After Elimelech and her sons died, Ruth returned to Bethlehem as a widow. She had no children or grandchildren to ensure her legacy or provide for her. A woman's security came from her father, her husband, and her sons. Naomi was grieving, so she asked her friends to call her Mara ("bitter").

Ways to Impact the World

Naomi was honest about the grief she was experiencing, even to the point of asking her friends to call her by another name. Being honest means telling the truth in a straightforward and sincere way. Naomi had experienced extreme loss – losing her husband and two sons. One of her daughters-in-law (Orpah) abandoned her in favor of returning to her family and gods. She returned to Bethlehem after being away for years. (and I imagine that she was experiencing reverse culture shock.)

I've heard my friends say they're doing, "Fine" when in reality their lives fell to pieces. Talking about emotions in a healthy and appropriate way (not gossiping!) will help tremendously in the grief process. Believe it or not, God wants to be involved in every aspect of our lives. He already knows how we're feeling and what we're experiencing. His arms are open wide to help us.

God never left Naomi. He answered the cry of her heart. Through her family (Ruth, Boaz, and their son, Obed), the Lord restored her life and nourished her in her old age (Ruth 4:15).

10. Hannah – Commitment to Prayer

Hannah was one of the two wives of Elkanah. His other wife, Peninnah had children but Hannah didn't because the Lord closed her womb (1 Samuel 1:1-2, 5). Elkanah gave Hannah a double portion. Peninnah was Hannah's rival and made her life miserable (1 Samuel 1:6). Jealousy and rivalry can make life difficult, and this went on year after year (1 Samuel 1:7). Hannah had the favor of her husband, but did not have children.

Hannah prayed to the Lord and wept bitterly. I imagine all the pain in her heart came flowing out as she threw herself on the care of the Lord. All the frustration from her family situation and, perhaps, feeling like a failure as a wife for not providing children for her husband was put at the feet of God. She asked God to not forget her and to give her a son! She promised that she would dedicate the child to the Lord's service (1 Samuel 1:11). Eli the priest thought she was drunk and reprimanded her. Hannah told him that she was "speaking out of her great anxiety and vexation." (1 Samuel 1:16) God answered Hannah's prayer and gave her a son, Samuel, which means "heard of God" (1 Samuel 1:20). Once Samuel was weaned, Hannah brought him to the House of the Lord at Shiloh (1 Samuel 1:25-28) and brought her son. She gave her son to Eli for service to the Lord.

Ways to Impact the World

Do you pray? Do you communicate with God about your problems and concerns? Do you offer God thanks and praise for the blessings He has given you? Hannah brought her pain and heartbreak to the Lord. She offers her praise to Him in

1 Samuel 2:1-10. She praises Him with all her strength and rejoices in His salvation.

When you pray, you can experience God's heart.

11. Abigail – Diplomacy[11]

When we first meet Abigail (1 Samuel 25:1-44), she is married to a man named Nabal. She is described as "discerning and beautiful" but her husband was "harsh and badly behaved." Someone who is discerning is perceptive, astute, and shrewd.

David sent his servants to Nabal and asked him for food. Nabal was very rude to the servants and sent them away without any refreshment! We've talked before about the importance of hospitality in biblical times. Nabal was insulting David and his men on many levels! David was ready to get retribution against Nabal. Abigail put together food and drink and rushed out to meet David's men. She very diplomatically dealt with her husband's rudeness. Later, Nabal passed away and Abigail married David.

Ways to Impact the World

Abigail showed wisdom in how she handled a very difficult situation. She made reparations for her husband and saved everyone from pain and suffering.

The book of Proverbs is full of solid wisdom: "A gentle answer turns away wrath, but a harsh word stirs up anger." (15:1).

Abigail demonstrated how to effectively handle a difficult situation in a sensitive way

- She acknowledged the situation – Abigail heard about her

---

11   http://www.christiananswers.net/dictionary/abigail.html

husband's behavior. There would be consequences. She acknowledged the gravity of the situation!

- She smoothed the way – Abigail prepared food and drink for David and his men.

- She apologized to David – apologized for her husband's behavior and asked for forgiveness.

Pray for wisdom in how to handle difficult situations with grace and tact. We can impact the world by sharing God's grace with people around us.

12. Queen Esther – Compassion

Hadassah (which means "compassion") is the Hebrew name of a jewish woman who would become Queen Esther of Persia. (The name Esther means "star".) Esther was raised by her cousin Mordecai, one of the Israelites carried out of Jerusalem as a captive into Babylon (2:6). Mordecai stayed true to his jewish faith. (For example, he refused to bow down to the prime minister, Haman (3:2). I imagine Mordecai telling Esther about the life he lived in Jerusalem and how frustrating it was to live cross-culturally.

Esther's life took an unexpected turn when she was brought into the King's harem (2:8). She won the favor of the king (2:17) and he made her queen. The wicked Haman was angry at Mordecai for snubbing him so he plotted to have all the jewish people in the kingdom killed. Esther revealed herself as a jewish woman, foiled Haman's plot, and saved her people from certain destruction.

Esther found herself in a perilous position when Mordecai revealed Haman's plot to kill their people. Esther's response was to fast and pray before she went to the king to save her people. She famously said, "…if I perish, I perish." (4:16)

Ways to Impact the World

I've never had the responsibility of intervening for a whole group of people in danger of certain death. My life has never been threatened. It is difficult to imagine being in her precarious position. Esther was motivated by love and compassion. Unless she intervened, her people would perish.

I have intervened in situations where people and their lives was spiraling out of control. I was motivated by showing and extending the kindness of God.

Compassion is when we're moved to action by the pain of another person, especially someone who is vulnerable. Your response to the needs of others is a powerful way to impact the world.

13. Elizabeth - Friendship

In the beginning of the book of Luke, we are introduced to a priest named Zechariah and his wife Elisabeth (Like 1:5). They are described as righteous, or blameless, before God. They followed the commandments of God found in the book of the Law. However, like other couples in the Bible (like Abraham & Sarah), they didn't have children and they were getting up in years. Zechariah was chosen to go into the Holy of Holies to minister before the Lord. Once a year, a priest would go into the Holy of Holies where the Spirit of the Lord dwelled on Earth. God told Zechariah that his prayers would be answered and Elisabeth would have a son! Elisabeth conceived a son and gave birth to John, the messenger of the coming of Christ.

Mary, the mother of Jesus came to visit Elisabeth during their pregnancies. John leaped in Elizabeth's womb when he heard Mary's voice. Elisabeth praises Mary by saying, "And blessed is she who believed that there would be a fulfilment of what is spoken to her from the Lord."

Ways to Impact the World

Over the years I have been blessed to have friends who loved me through difficult times, encouraged me, and prayed for me. As women, we need each other. Having friends to accompany us through transitions creates bonds that last a lifetime. Don't minimize the power of time with the women God brings into your life.

Women go through a lot of transitions (both positive and

negative) like marriage, motherhood, divorce, and widowhood. We can show God's grace to each other by supporting our sisters in Christ in all of life's changes.

14. Mary – The Mother of Jesus – Obedience

We've talked about a few mothers who conceived under unusual circumstances or against the odds. Sarah laughed when she heard she'd become a mother at 90 (Genesis 18:12). The Lord gave Hannah a son after years of not conceiving (1 Samuel 1:1-27, 2:1-33). The husbands of women who conceived in the most unlikely circumstances had their own responses. For example, Zechariah responded to the angel Gabriel with doubt (Luke 1:18).

Mary the Mother of Jesus[12] was from Nazareth, a backwater town in northern Israel (Luke 1:26). She was a young woman (I've heard people say she was between ages 12-16) and had a common name. The Lord calls her "favored one" (1:28). She was chosen to carry the son of God! Mary was greatly troubled (1:29), which is completely understandable. Her response to Gabriel's news was, "Behold, I am the servant of the Lord; let it be to me according to your word." (1:38)

Ways to Impact the World

If the angel of the Lord came down to me the spectrum of my responses would run from shock to complete disbelief. I'd say something along the lines of, "Yeah, right!"

I don't know if Mary really understood the weight of her decision. The child that grew in her womb, kicked, grew and developed, would save the world. She nursed him and watched him learn to walk. When Mary and Joseph carried Jesus into the temple to be dedicated, Simeon told her, "Behold, this child is appointed

---

12 https://en.wikipedia.org/wiki/Mary_%28mother_of_Jesus%29

for the fall and rising of many in Israel…" (Luke 2:34) Being the mother of Jesus would cause her great pain as well (Luke 2:35).

Because of Mary's obedience, the Redeemer of the world was born. The actions of Adam and Eve brought sin into the world and separated us from God. Jesus created a bridge so we can return to God! Mary's obedience had a long reaching impact on the world.

I have impacted the lives of many pastoring with my husband, as a community educator—teaching phonics, writing and producing cds, dvds, books while promoting the fine arts in a Christian venue.

What can an act of obedience allow God to do through you?

Saying, "Yes" to God is something you'll never regret.

15. Anna – Patience

Anna's story appears in the book of Luke when Jesus is presented at the Temple (Luke 2:36-38). Anna was married and widowed at a young age without children. She spent her entire life in the temple worshiping God with continual fasting and prayer. Anna was 84 years old when Jesus was born. She recognized Jesus for who He was and gave thanks to God because the redemption of Israel finally arrived.

Ways to Impact the World

It is clear that Anna was a devout Jew. After she lost her husband, she spent decades in the Temple where God dwelled. At the time of Jesus' birth, Israel was invaded by the Romans. The Israelites were under oppression. I imagine that Anna prayed for her people and for the promised coming King. Jesus was Israel's Redeemer and He came to restore Israel. Anna had the privilege of sharing the news that Israel's redeemer arrived.

What is something you've prayed for and longed for and longed for?

You can move mountains and change the world through prayer.

16. Bathsheba – Processing Loss

The Story of David and Bathsheba is pretty sordid (1 Samuel 11:1-27, 12:1-31). King David initiated an affair with Bathsheba, a married woman and she became pregnant. To cover up Bathsheba's pregnancy, David first tried getting Bathsheba's husband, Uriah, to sleep with her. He refused so David sent him to the frontlines. Over the next few months, Bathsheba became a widow and David married her. The child she gave birth to died.

We know from the beginning of 1 Samuel 11 that David wasn't where he was supposed to be – instead of going down to battle, he stayed at home (vs. 1). He saw a beautiful woman bathing from his roof (vs. 2). At any point in this series of events, David could've stop things from happening.

Ways to Impact the World

It's easy to make assumptions about Bathsheba's character from the story and that's not the focus. Bathsheba experienced great loss as a result of the whole situation. My heart breaks for her as a wife losing her husband in the violence of battle and a mother who loses an infant son. She then married the man who caused her husband's death.

What I see in Bathsheba is a woman who had to process great loss.[13]

Grief is an important process we go through to deal with loss of different kinds. I don't know if Bathsheba loved Uriah. He served in the military so they were apart for periods of time. He acknowledged the value of respecting the Lord (11:11).

---

13 http://www.webmd.com/balance/tc/grief-and-grieving-what-happens

Maybe she contemplated the reality of losing her husband in battle, but certainly not under such awful circumstances.

The grief process[14] isn't neat and tidy.

1. Denial – rejecting the idea that the tragedy or loss even happened

2. Anger – strong emotions of frustration or resentment. It can be directed toward ourselves, other people, or the Lord.

3. Bargaining – trying to negotiate for a change in circumstances

4. Depression – feeling of hopelessness over the loss

5. Acceptance – coming to terms with the loss or tragedy

Loss and grief are difficult and it takes time to process everything that comes with a tragic event.

God's spirit is always with us in all circumstances.

---

14 http://grief.com/the-five-stages-of-grief/

17. A Sinful Woman Forgiven[15] – Repentance

Jesus did not shy away from spending time with social and spiritual outcasts like tax collectors and prostitutes. He went to people who were lost and broken because, "…I have not come to call the righteous, but sinners." (Mark 2:17). In Luke 7:36-50, Jesus is invited to have dinner in the house of a Pharisee, or Jewish religious leader. A woman identified as a "sinner" entered the house. We don't know what her specific sin is, but she's got a bad reputation.

The sinful woman washed Jesus' feet with her tears and wiped them with her hair. She anointed his feet with ointment, a precious commodity. Jesus contrasts her actions with his host, Simon. Simon did not follow the tradition of offering hospitable gestures to guests like washing the dust of travel from their feet. The sinful woman demonstrated great love for Christ through her actions.

Ways to Impact the World

The Pharisees were religious leaders and followed strict guidelines for their own spiritual purity. This story shows strong contrast between this leader and a woman who was considered a sinner. The woman demonstrated greater commitment to Him than a religious leader.

Jesus tells the woman her sins are forgiven (Luke 7:48). The Word says that all have sinned and fall short of God's glory (Romans 3:23). The more we read the bible and get to know the Lord, the more we can see the dire situation that Christ's death saved us from. The sinful woman humbled herself before the Lord. Her actions touched Christ's heart because she was genuine.

---

15 https://en.wikipedia.org/wiki/Parable_of_the_Two_Debtors

18. Samaritan woman at the well – One encounter can change everything

My heart resonates with the Samaritan woman at the well (John 4:1-45) because it shows how gently Jesus treated women and how one encounter with Him can change everything. Jesus was traveling through Samaria (4:4), the land adjacent to Israel. Samaritans were considered to be second class citizens (4:9). Jesus sat at the well and asked a woman who came to draw water for a drink of water. Jesus offers the woman living water (4:13) and they will never be thirsty again. After Jesus' encounter with the woman, she went home and told the people in Samaria her testimony and many people believed in Him (4:39).

Ways to Impact the World

I find it discouraging how harsh we can be on women. The woman in this story was living with a man she wasn't married to (4:16-17). I don't want to speculate on why she wasn't married; her living situation was not culturally condoned.

Jesus showed the woman compassion instead of condemnation. He offered her living water, the source of eternal life. Things would've gone very differently if Jesus said, "Your behavior is disgusting."

I grew up with two Christian parents. As much as my parents loved the Lord, they were not perfect. My Dad would often cut off affection and ignore me if I behaved in a way he disapproved of. I learned that love was based on my ability to perform. I projected that onto the Lord for a long time. I felt like God would reject me if I failed Him. From this story, I learned that Christ calls us to Himself by offering hope and life. The more I realize that, the more feel I free to serve Him – without feeling like I have to perform to an impossible standard.

The woman returned to her town and told everyone the story of her encounter. She didn't keep Jesus' living water to herself! She made sure to share His story with others.

One encounter with Christ in our lives can bring forgiveness and new life.

Mary & Martha

The sisters Mary and Martha, sisters of Lazarus, are often treated as a pair. I don't want to minimize either's character so I'm addressing them separately. Jesus loved Martha, Mary, and Lazarus (John 11:4). They lived in Bethany, two miles from Jerusalem (John 11:18). What I see in the lives of Mary and Martha is:

- Jesus loves all of us (John 11:4)

- The gifts everyone brings with them has value.

- We have to find balance in areas of life and ministry. Christians have to sit at Christ's feet as well as serve others.

19. Mary, the sister of Lazarus – Listening to the Word

Luke 10:38-41 tells the story of Jesus visiting Mary and Martha in their home. While Jesus was there, Mary sat at the feet of Jesus and listened to what He had to say (10:39). Mary's decision to sit at the feet of God and listening to His teachings is called "the good portion."

Ways to Impact the World

Relying on God for our daily sustenance is a way to impact the world.

Different parts of the world have different staple foods as the basis for their diet. In some regions of Papua New Guinea, it is sweet potatoes. In some Asian countries, rice is the basis for daily diet. Our bodies need daily nourishment in order to function. Without food, our energy level fades, we can't focus, and we can get downright cranky.

In the Lord's Prayer (Matthew 6:9-13), Jesus instructs us to ask for our daily bread (vs. 11). What Christ is referring to is spiritual food from time we spend with Him that feeds the soul. Regularly spending time with Him will prevent Spiritual malnourishment or starvation.

Listening to the Word and studying it will encourage our spiritual growth. Without being fed, we'll become spiritually anemic.

- Read the Word and study it on a daily basis – The Bible is our Daily Bread and our connection to God's heart.

The Bible has instructions for all of life's situations. Additionally, try listening to the Word – I recommend getting a bible app like Faith Comes by Hearing so you can *listen* to the Word while you're driving or doing chores. Reading a different translation than you're used to can help you see a verse in a different way.

- Listen to teaching and preaching – Pastors, priests, and other biblical teachers have the responsibility of helping christians apply the Word to their lives.

- Use bible study tools and books to help you understand how to apply the Scripture to your life. At different times in my life I have benefitted from studies specifically for women and for dealing with family relationships.

There are times in our lives when we need to set aside the pressures of our lives and make sure to sit at Christ's feet. Daily quiet time is necessary for our minds and bodies to experience the necessary rest and refreshment.

20. Martha, the sister of Lazarus – Working Together in Ministry

When Jesus visited Mary and Martha, Martha stepped into the role of host. She was responsible for making sure their guest had enough food and drink (Luke 10:40). Martha became frustrated with Mary for not helping to provide for their guest's needs. Jesus notices that Martha is "anxious and troubled about many things" (11:41).

Ways to Impact the World

Martha was following the cultural standards of the day by making sure that everyone in her home was comfortable. If Jesus came to visit, other people from Bethany would show up to visit, too. She was focused on making sure everything was ready.

I've learned a lot the past few years about how much work and how many individuals are required to make a ministry project happen. (I can really identify with Martha's frustration!)

All kinds of ministry require people to work together. I've learned that working on a team requires some things:

- Patience – Working together means making sure everyone is "on the same page" as far as goals and communication. It takes time, sure, but we have to put other peoples' needs first.

- Common purpose – Everyone on the team has to be working for a specific goal.

- God gives everyone different gifts and all are important. It would be silly to expect one person to design a set, run a sound board, prepare refreshments, and preach a message. Respect the gifts of others and remember that you have something to offer, too.

Working on a team for common goals gives us a small taste of how the Body of Christ functions.

21. The Woman Caught in Adultery – Redemption

John 8:1-11 tells the story of Jesus and a woman caught in adultery. Jesus was sitting on the steps of the Temple, an important place where religious discussions took place. The religious leaders of the day (the Scribes and the Pharisees) decided that they would test Jesus in a very public way (vs. 6) at the expense of a young woman's life. They brought a woman who was caught in adultery to Jesus (vs. 3). I don't know anything about this woman; I just imagine her in a vulnerable position with her hair in a mess, may be partially dressed. She knew that the consequence of her actions was to be executed by stoning. She would be taken to the outside of the city and would die of blunt force trauma in a painful and humiliating way.

Jesus knew the book of the Law as well. Leviticus 20:10 says that both a man and a woman found in adultery should be punished, but only the woman was brought. (Where was the man she was caught with?) The religious leaders approached Jesus and asked him what they should do (vs. 5). Jesus bent down and wrote with his finger in the dust. I don't think the fact that Jesus was writing is important; what I do think is important is the fact that he was looking up at the woman instead of looking down on her. He says the person without sin should cast the first stone. If anyone in that situation was qualified, it was Jesus Himself, because He was without sin. The accusers all walked away from the woman. Jesus tells her to go and sin no more.

Ways to Impact the World

What set Jesus apart from the revered religious leaders was his *compassion.* I am continually amazed at how he treated people who were societies' outcasts and victims. He did not throw this woman out of the city to be killed; instead He told her to live her life free from sin.

What happened to her? Did she go home and begin living a life to honor God? Did she get married, have a family, and follow the Lord? Did she walk past the temple and see the people who accused her? We meet this woman at what is most likely the lowest point in her life.

Jesus gives us all a second chance to live a positive life for His glory. He is full of compassion especially for those who are vulnerable and lost.

This precious woman walked away with a second chance and the directive, "Go and sin no more." (8:11)

22. Mary Magdalene – Telling your story[16]

Mary Magdalene the name of a woman found in all four Gospels. She was from the town of Magdala on the Sea of Galilee. In Mark 16:9, she is healed and delivered from seven evil spirits. What a power testimony of transition from possession to freedom!

Jesus and the disciples were traveling through cities and villages sharing the Good News of the Kingdom of God. They were accompanied by women: Mary Magdalene, Joanna, and Susana. These women provided financial support for Jesus and the disciples (Luke 8:1-3). Mary Magdalene was there to witness the gruesome spectacle of a public execution of Jesus by crucifixion (Mark 15:40-41). She was there to witness the burial of Jesus in the tomb (Matthew 27:61). She went back to the tomb to anoint his body with spices and spoke with the angel of the Lord (Matthew 28:1, 5-7). She was the first to see Jesus after he rose from the dead (Mark 16:9) and shared the story with the disciples who didn't believe.

Ways to Impact the World

Mary Magdalene's life can provide us guidelines and insight about a life of ministry. Mary Magdalene devoted her life to serving Jesus and following him after she had a powerful encounter - being delivered from seven demons! She experienced freedom from bondage because of Jesus crossing her path! Mary Magdalene was with a group of women who traveled with the disciples. This could very possibly be the first women's ministry. Crowds gathered around Jesus wherever He was. They came asking for

[16] http://www.crosswalk.com/family/singles/the-women-in-christs-life-mary-magdalene-1380353.html

healing, out of curiosity, or to hear His teaching. She was there witnessing the defining events of Christianity - Christ dying on the cross and rising from the dead. To be a witness simply means to tell what you know and what you've experienced.

Here are some insights about women's ministry that we can glean from Mary Magdalene's story:

- God has the power to deliver us from evil in all forms. An encounter with Him sets us free.

- In order to minister to people, you have to meet with them. Mary Magdalene traveled with Jesus through different cities. She came in contact with different individuals from different walks of life.

- People who share the Good News need financial support! Tithe your income to your local church or a ministry of your choice.

23. The Woman with the Issue of Blood – Faith

The woman with the issue of blood came to Jesus when he was on his way to heal the daughter of a ruler, Jarius (Matthew 9:18-26, Luke 5:22). The woman approached Jesus while he was going to the ruler's house along with his disciples. Wherever Jesus went, he was surrounded by people who were crowding in to touch him, ask for healing, or listen to his teachings (Luke 5:24).

The woman is presented (Matthew 9:20) as having suffered from a discharge of blood for twelve years. Menstruation can make women feel bloated, weak, uncomfortable, moody, and experiencing painful cramps. This woman had a continuous menstrual flow for twelve years. The woman had spent all of her income on doctors trying to find a cure for her illness (Mark 6:26). The fact that she was bleeding made her and anyone who touched her ceremonially unclean (Leviticus 15:19-33). She told herself, "If I could only touch his garment I will be made well." (Matthew 9:20). She had so much confidence in Jesus that she believed touching the edge of his clothing would be enough to restore her health (Luke 5:28).

Ways to Impact the World

Jesus put people first and he showed this woman great compassion and understanding. He did not condemn her for being unclean. This woman came to Jesus out of faith. When she touched Him, she was immediately healed.

Jesus wore the garment of a Jewish man as commanded in the book of Numbers. Jesus came to fulfil the Law and the Prophets (Matthew 5:17). By reaching out and touching the cords on the corner of Christ's garment, the woman with the issue of blood was acknowledging His Lordship. All of the promises of God found in the Law were there for her if she would reach out.

Christ wants us to acknowledge His Lordship with our whole heart. Faith flows from a heart that acknowledges who God is and a heart that puts its trust in Him. One single touch from Him restores us.

24. Lydia[17] - An Open Heart

Lydia is mentioned in the book of Acts 16:11-15. She met Paul and Silas in Philippi during their third missionary journey. According to Acts 16:14, she sold purple goods (scholars believe she was either a merchant or worked with textiles) and she worshiped God. On the Sabbath, Paul and Silas met a group of women on the riverside outside the city (vs. 13). The Lord opened Lydia's heart (vs. 14) as she was listening to Paul's words. Her whole family was baptized (vs. 14) and she asked the missionaries to come stay with her family. Paul and Silas visited Lydia again when they were released from the Philippian jail (vs. 40) before traveling on to Thessalonica.

Ways to Impact the World

Some biblical characters who encountered the apostles on their missionary journeys are only given a few verses of mention. The encounters of Paul and Silas are briefly described in Acts. Lydia is identified by her occupation ("she sold purple goods") and that she worshiped God (Acts 16:14). What is especially notable about Lydia is that her heart was open to God!

As you look back on your life, how has God prepared you to impact the world. What can you do now?.

- Pray for God to bring men and women who love Him into your life to mentor you through different circumstances.

- Read books about the christian life.

---

17   http://www.womeninthescriptures.com/2011/03/lydia.html

- Ask God to show you ways that you need to grow personally.

When we ask God to meet us where we are, we will begin to see Him in our lives.

25. Tabitha[18] - Acts of service

The name Tabitha means "gazelle" and in Greek it is Dorcas. She is introduced as a disciple in Acts 9:35. Disciple is from the root word discipline which means to learn. Tabitha lived in Joppa (or Jaffa), a city in Israel, and was "full of food works and acts of charity" (9:36). Her charity included making tunics and other garments. She did this to provide for those in need (9:39). While Peter was in Lydda (twelve miles from Joppa), Tabitha became sick and passed away (9:38). The disciples sent for Peter and asked him to come after Tabitha's death. The widows had placed her in an upper bedroom and the people there were weeping and mourning. They were showing all of the clothing that Tabitha had made for them. Peter came to where Tabitha was laid out. Peter took her hand and raised her from the dead (9:40)

Ways to Impact the World

As I read this passage, I find myself wondering why did Peter raise Tabitha from the dead? She was known for her generosity and service to others. She worked hard to meet the needs of others. Insight is found in vs. 42: "…and many believed in the Lord." Peter raised Tabitha from the dead in order to bring glory to God.

Tabitha demonstrated the spiritual gift of acts of service (Romans 12:7) I've known a lot of beautiful Christian women like Tabitha who worked to meet the physical needs of others. We can do the same thing. There are so many opportunities to help meet the needs of people that need help.

---
18 http://www.womeninthescriptures.com/2011/07/tabithadorcus.html

I believe that God calls us to reach out to the world and show His love. Not everyone has the opportunity to travel overseas because of health, family commitments, and work duties. However, we can serve wherever we are! A lot of missionary work involves preparing the way for others to hear about Christ through acts of service. As a willing worker myself I've seen how communities respond when folks come and make sure the village or city has clean water or trained teachers or medical care. When people know that you care and are invested in them they are more likely to listen to the gospel.

A lot of churches offer ministry opportunities for you to serve others using your gifts and talents. There may be an already existing ministry like:

- A food kitchen or pantry that provides nourishment for local families.

- Vacation Bible School for the children in a community.

- Donate used clothing and toys for the children's ministry.

Thinking outside the box, what are some ways you can also be creative about how you use your talents for God?

- If you are an accountant you can offer budgeting classes.

- If you know how to cut hair you can offer back to school haircuts for children.

- There are many opportunities to serve in different capacities to glorify God and impact the world.

WOMAN TO WOMAN MINISTRIES

A bleak world,
Engulfed in despair.
Crisis, hatred, bloodshed,
Brokenness everywhere.

Divided personalities…divided people,
Secure in isolation,
We need to belong…yet
So much alienation.

Incapable of loving ourselves and others,
From God alienated.
Incapacitated by sin and flesh,
From God separated.

People with feelings of desolation—
Depression, anxiety, frustration,
People bound by trepidation.
Is there any consolation?

Woman to woman ministries
For such a time as this.
Overcoming barriers to build
God's opportunists!!!

Passionate pillars of purpose,
Building in every respect,
Lives carefully repaired,
Making them God's elect.

Worthy to be praised—
Women that fear the Lord,
Mobilizing human resources,
Suggesting one accord.

Born and burdened to one end
Proclaiming the Good News.
With a holy spiritual fervor,
Challenging alternate views.

Women of faith, mourning women
In prayer they travail.
Women of humility, cunning women
In service they prevail.

Woman to woman ministries,
Meeting needs is a must.
Patiently teaching others
In God we trust.

Thank God for:
Women so fair!
Women so rare!
Women that share!
Women that dare!

OH WOMAN OF MINISTRY

Oh woman, oh woman of ministry
Who does require,
Such dedication and commitment
Is it fair to inquire, or not?
All of a sudden…from the rear
From your assigned place,
To the vanguard of ministry---
To the forefront of the race.

You're action oriented,
Are motives ulterior?
You're goal directed
Are purposes superior.
We thought that ministry
Has always been
The private domain
Of God sent men.

The whole world is shocked
Not only about sins,
Or angry spirit led men
But by current trends.
So many women
Now women out of the home!
Now women running government!
Now women running businesses!
Now women running churches!
By what authority?

Stop the women, stop the women

Before its too late,
They're taking over everywhere
Even in the state.
Can God use a woman
To tell men?
Yes Jesus did,
"Go tell the brethren."

God uses whomever,
He pleases,
It'll be that way
Until time ceases.
Who am I..to question
God's acts,
It's in the book
All of the facts.
Father knows best.

Oh woman, Oh woman of ministry
Be genuine…be real,
Surmount your obstacles
Do God's will.
Seek to please Him.

FORTHCOMING BOOKS BY ELEANOR CRAWFORD:

WOMEN: 25 FACTS ABOUT WOMEN

WOMEN: 25 WOMEN THAT CHANGED HISTORY

WOMEN OF DESTINY: 25 CHALLENGES

WOMEN OF WISDOM: 25 INSIGHTS

WOMEN'S RESOURCES: 25 ASSETS

WOMEN'S MANUAL: 25 LIFE LESSONS

WOMEN'S WORKBOOK: 25 ACTIVITIES

WOMEN'S QUIZ BOOK

WOMEN'S DEVOTIONAL BOOK

WOMEN'S AFFIRMATION BOOK

WOMEN'S SERMONS: 25 SERMONS

WOMEN AND MEN: 25 CONTRASTS

FORTHCOMING BOOKS BY ALPHONSO CRAWFORD

LIFE'S WAY UNTIL: POEMS ON FAITH/HOPE/SALVATION

TWO HEARTS: LOVE POEMS/LOVE LETTERS

CROSSROADS: POEMS ON RACE/POLITICS/LIFE

100 WAYS FOR PEOPLE TO GET HEALED

100 SYMBOLS OF HEALTH AND HEALING

ADVANCED HEALING MANUAL

TRIUMPHANT: 25 WAYS TO EXCEL IN LIFE

THE THREE GREATEST CHALLENGES OF LIFE

DOMINATE: 25 DOMINION PRINCIPLES

WHY GOD MADE BLACK PEOPLE BLACK: 25 REASONS WHY

WISDOM PERSPECTIVES: 25 INSIGHTS

WISDOM: 25 FACTS ABOUT WISDOM

WISDOM ILLUSTRATED

LEADERSHIP IN AN AGE OF CRISIS:

25 OBSERVATIONS

LEADERSHIP: 25 FACTS ABOUT LEADERS

LEADERSHIP: 25 PITFALLS/POWERTOOLS

LEADERSHIP: 25 TOUGH QUESTIONS/TOUGH ANSWERS

DREAMS: 25 FEATURES

GOD'S WILL: 25 WAYS TO KNOW GOD'S WILL FOR YOUR LIFE

ADVANCED INTERPERSONAL COMMUNICATION: 25 EXPRESSIONS

POWERS THAT WOMEN POSSESS

POWER: 25 FACTS ABOUT POWER

SPIRITUOTHERAPY: 25 PRINCIPLES

THE POWER OF BIG THINKING: 25 LAWS

HEALTH AND HEALING QUIZ BOOK

HEALTH AND HEALING DEVOTIONAL BOOK

HEALTH AND HEALING BOOK OF AFFIRMATIONS

HEALTH AND HEALING SCRIPTURES

HEALTH AND HEALING WORKBOOK: 25 ACTIVITIES

HEART: 25 FACTS ABOUT THE HEART

BLOOD: 25 FACTS ABOUT BLOOD

MEN: 25 FACTS ABOUT MEN

PERSONALITY PROFILES: A BIBLICAL PERSPECTIVE

MY OWN WORST ENEMY: THE MANY WAYS WE LIE TO OURSELVES EVERYDAY

LORD WHY: CRITICAL QUESTIONS REGARDING MY FAITH

HEALTH AND HEALING: 25 HEALTH AND HEALING SERMONS

FORTHCOMING BOOKS BY BYRON CRAWFORD

SELL YOUR WAY TO SUCCESS: 25 WAYS TO SUCCEED IN LIFE:

SUCCESS IN LIFE: 25 STEPS TO THE TOP

LAWS OF SUCCESS: 25 PRINCIPLES

SUCCESS SECRETS: 25 INSIGHTS

SYNONYMS FOR SUCCESS: 25 CORRELATIONS

SUCCESS MANUAL: 25 LIFE LESSONS

SUCCESS WORKBOOK: 25 POWERFUL ACTIVITIES

SUCCESSFUL STRATEGIC PLANNING:

25 TACTICS

SUCCESS QUIZ BOOK

SUCCESS SERMONS: 25 SERMONS

SUCCESS DEVOTIONAL BOOK

SUCCESS AFFIRMATION BOOK

SIGN UP AND BE NOTIFIED FOR
SEMINARS/WORKSHOPS/CONFERENCES

NAME_____

ADDRESS_____
_____

CITY_____

STATE_____ZIP CODE_____

PHONE NO._____

EMAIL ADDRESS_____
_____

SEND TO:
NEW LIFE EDUCATIONAL SERVICES
P.O. BOX 96
OAK LAWN, ILLINOIS 60454

SEMINARS/WORKSHOPS/CONFERENCES

- ANNUAL WOMENS' CONFERENCE
- HEALTH AND HEALING
- DREAMS AND VISIONS
- PERSONAL POWER
- GIFTS AND TALENTS
- RELATIONSHIPS
- PROBLEM SOLVING
- HOW TO START A BUSINESS
- PERSONALITY PROFILES
- FIVEFOLD MINISTRY
- INTERPRETING CURRENT TRENDS
- ADVANCED STRATEGIC PLANNING
- ADVANCED INTERPERSONAL COMMUNICATION
- MANAGING SELF
- MANAGING CONFLICT
- MANAGING STRESS

- LAWS OF POWER
- ANNUAL MENS' CONFERENCE
- NEGOTIATION SKILLS
- BIG THINKING POWER
- STRATEGIES FOR SUCCESS
- HOW TO SELL YOURSELF
- THE DYNAMICS OF PURPOSE
- GLOBAL STEWARDSHIP
- HOW TO COUNSEL
- SELF MOTIVATION
- PEOPLE MOTIVATION
- SPIRITUAL EXERCISES
- NEGOTIATION SKILLS
- LIFE SKILLS
- TEAM BUILDING
- HOW TO START A CHRISTIAN SCHOOL
- HOW TO HOME SHOOL

- LIFE SKILLS
- NEEDS OF WOMEN AND MEN
- MARRIAGE RENEWAL
- CHALLENGING CHALLENGES
- WEALTH IN YOU
- LIFE LONG LEARNING
- APOSTOLIC/PROPHETIC CONFERENCE
- SETTING GOALS
- SELF DECEPTION: HOW WE LIE TO OURSELVES EVERYDAY
- FEEDBACK
- HOW TO BECOME A CONSULTANT
- TIME MANAGEMENT
- CHANGE AGENTS
- VISION

ABOUT THE AUTHOR

Eleanor has remarkable leadership skills. She is an outstanding speaker that projects all the sophistication, graces, and charms of an ambassador of Christ. Women are encouraged to

passionately pursue their dreams while they engage themselves in kingdom ministry. Eleanor pastors with her husband at Cathedral of Prayer.

Eleanor has a Bachelor of Arts Degree from Chicago State University, a Master of Divinity and Doctor of Ministry from Cathedral Theological Seminary.

Her goals are directed towards one end, fulfilling the spiritual mandate that God has given her.

"John 9:4..I must work the works of Him that sent me, while it is day; the night cometh when no man can work."

"Ephesians 2:10..For we are His workmanship, created in Christ Jesus unto good works, which God hath before ordained that we should walk in them."

"Philippians 1:6..Being confident of this very thing, that He which hath begun a good work in you will perform it until the day of Jesus Christ".

"Philippians 2:12-13..Wherefore my beloved, as ye have always obeyed, not as in my presence only,

but now much more in my absence, work out your own salvation in fear and trembling.

For it is God which worketh in you both to will and to do of His good pleasure."

"John 14:12..Verily, verily, I say unto you, He that

believeth on me, the works that I do shall he do also; and greater works than these shall he do; because I go unto my Father.

www.ingramcontent.com/pod-product-compliance
Lightning Source LLC
Chambersburg PA
CBHW060419050426
42449CB00009B/2035